Beanstalk's Basics for Piano

LESSON BOOK
PREPARATORY
LEVEL A

by Cheryl Finn & Eamonn Morris

WILLIS MUSIC

EXCLUSIVELY DISTRIBUTED BY

HAL•LEONARD®
CORPORATION
7777 W. BLUEMOUND RD. P.O. BOX 13819 MILWAUKEE, WI 53213

CHERYL FINN

EAMONN MORRIS

12271

A NOTE TO PARENTS AND TEACHERS

Beanstalk's Basics for Piano uses a unique reward system to promote musical playing by the student at every level. Each piece of music is marked with a **Bravo Box** which highlights for the student certain specific elements required for a technically satisfying and musical performance of that piece. For each **Bravo Box** skill successfully mastered the teacher rewards the student with the matching colored sticker from the enclosed sticker sheet. The sticker is placed on the page to complete the illustration accompanying the music.

It is recommended that the teacher detach and retain the sticker sheet as the student begins each book. This preserves the element of surprise and increases motivation. Further, it ensures better control of the sticker allocation. Consideration of the **Bravo Box** and the sticker rewards for each piece is ideally withheld until the student has first mastered the basic elements of the music in question, including key signature, time signature, notes and rhythm.

Several of the pieces in **Beanstalk's Basics for Piano** contain a further learning tool called **Treasure Hunt**. Here the student is encouraged to search for answers to one or more technical questions about the piece and to provide these answers verbally to the teacher as part of a musical dialogue. This enjoyable exercise is designed to develop basic theory skills in a straightforward and practical way, and should be encouraged wherever indicated.

We wish much success to all students and teachers who find joy with us in making music musical!

Writing, Composition and Design:
Cheryl Finn and Eamonn Morris

Music Engraving:
Jim Littleford

Illustrations and Layout:
Jerrold Connors

Special Thanks to:
Angela Barbour and Jean Brown

This series is dedicated to our parents:

Glen & Dorrien Finn
and
Jim & Peggy Morris

AT THE PIANO

SITTING POSITION

1. Always make sure that your arms are level with or slightly higher than the keyboard. If your arms are lower than the keyboard, you will need to raise your sitting position by placing a cushion or book underneath you. If your feet do not touch the ground, it is also helpful to have a footstool for your feet to prevent them from dangling and to help you keep your balance.

2. Be sure that your elbows are held away from your sides and that your shoulders are always relaxed.

3. Sit up straight.

HAND POSITION

When you learn to play the piano it is very important that you play with a good hand position. Here are some things to remember...

1. Curve your fingers. Pretend that you have an orange in the palm of your

2. Be sure that your fingers are strong when you play and that you play with your finger tips.

3. A good hand position looks like this:

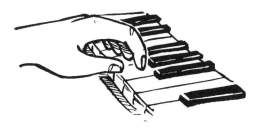

DID YOU KNOW THAT YOUR FINGERS HAVE NUMBERS?

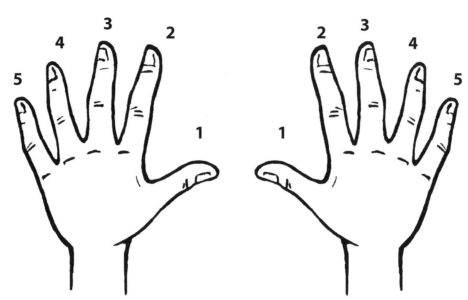

Trace your hands below and number your fingers.

Which is your **RIGHT HAND**? Color it **RED**. Which is your **LEFT HAND**? Color it **BLUE**.

12271

EXPLORING THE PIANO KEYBOARD

If you go **DOWN** the sounds are **LOWER**.

If you go **UP** the sounds are **HIGHER**.

KEYBOARD

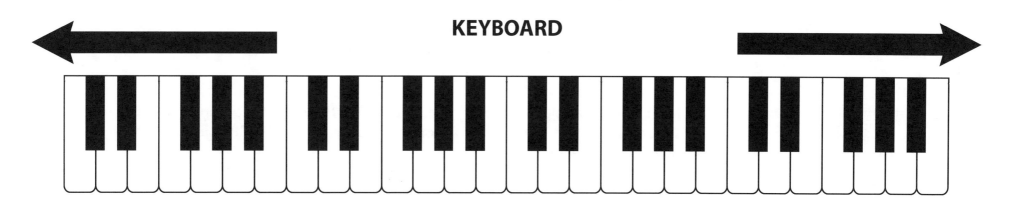

As you can see, the piano has
WHITE KEYS and **BLACK KEYS**.

The **BLACK KEYS** are divided into groups of **TWO** and **THREE**.

2

3

FUN WITH THE BLACK KEYS

Right Hand

1. Starting in the middle of the piano keyboard, place your **RIGHT HAND** on the **TWO BLACK KEYS** using fingers 2 and 3. Play the keys **TOGETHER**. Now play each group of two black keys **TOGETHER** going all the way **UP** to the top!

   Now play the two black keys **SEPARATELY** starting in the middle of the piano keyboard. First use finger 2, then 3. Go all the way **UP** to the top.

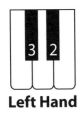

Left Hand

2. Starting in the middle of the piano keyboard, place your **LEFT HAND** on the **TWO BLACK KEYS** using fingers 2 and 3. Play the keys **TOGETHER**. Now play each group of two black keys **TOGETHER** going all the way **DOWN** to the bottom!

   Now play the keys **SEPARATELY**—first finger 2, then 3-all the way **DOWN** to the bottom. It's like taking your fingers for a walk!

Right Hand

3. Starting in the middle of the piano keyboard, place your **RIGHT HAND** on the group of **THREE BLACK KEYS**. Use fingers 2-3-4. Play each group of three black keys **TOGETHER** going all the way **UP** higher and higher to the top!

   Now play the keys **SEPARATELY** – first finger 2, then 3, then 4. Play all the groups of three black keys going **UP**!

Left Hand

4. Starting in the middle of the piano keyboard, place your **LEFT HAND** on the group of **THREE BLACK KEYS**. Use fingers 2-3-4. Play each group of three black keys **TOGETHER** going all the way **DOWN** lower and lower to the bottom!

   Now play the keys **SEPARATELY** – first finger 2, then 3, then 4. Play all the groups of three black keys all the way **DOWN** to the bottom!

12271

QUARTER NOTE

Music is made by different sounds. Some sounds are long and some sounds are short. We know to make the sound **SHORT** when we see a **QUARTER NOTE**. We give it **ONE** count.

Middle

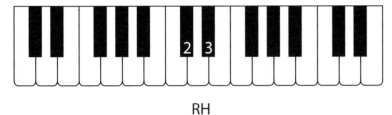

RH

Clap:

Count   1   2   3   4   1   2   3   4

BRAVO BOX

1. Good hand position

2. Steady tempo (speed) and counting

We use **BAR LINES** to divide the sounds into equal groups. These equal groups are called **MEASURES** or **BARS**.

We use a **DOUBLE BAR LINE** to show that it is **THE END** of the piece.

Bar Line   Double Bar Line

Measure   Measure

LET'S GO!

Try playing this on **ANY** group of **TWO BLACK KEYS** with **FINGERS 2 & 3** of your **RIGHT HAND**.

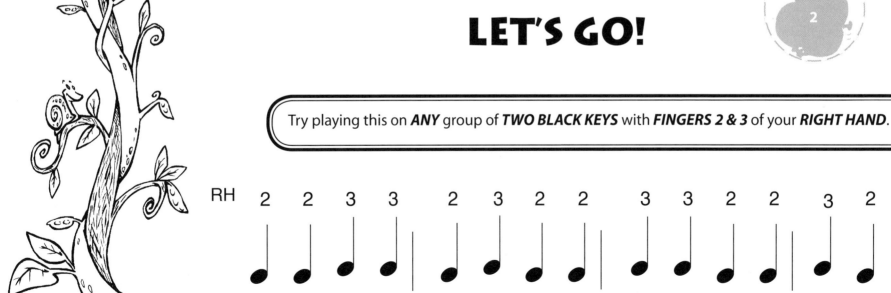

RH   2   2   3   3   2   3   2   2   3   3   2   2   3   2   3   3

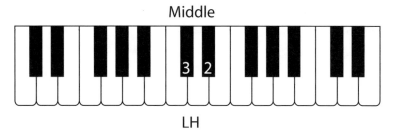

Middle

LH

BRAVO BOX

3. Good hand position

4. Steady tempo and counting

WHO'S THAT?

Try playing this on **ANY** group of **TWO BLACK KEYS** with **FINGERS 2 & 3** of your **LEFT HAND**.

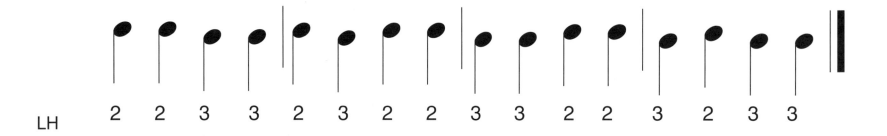

LH   2 2 3 3 2 3 2 2 3 3 2 2 3 2 3 3

A **HALF NOTE** is a **LONGER** note.
We give it **TWO** counts.

Clap:

Count: 1   2   3   4   1   2   3   4

Middle

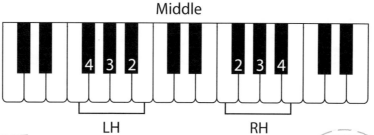

LH   RH

HALF NOTE TUNE

Try playing this on a group of **THREE BLACK KEYS** anywhere you like!

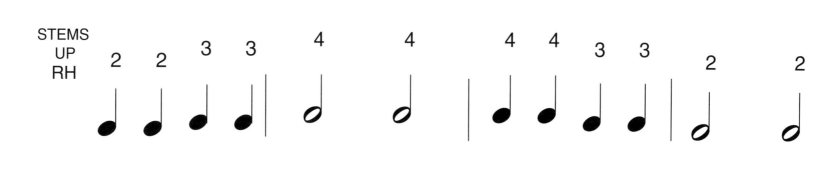

STEMS UP RH

STEMS DOWN LH

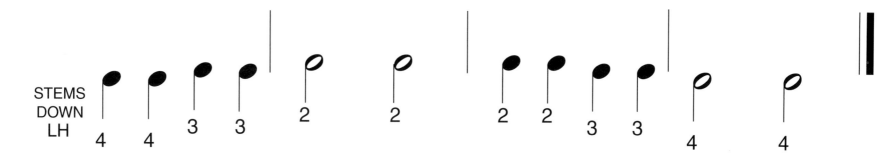

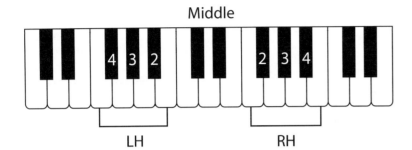

LH   RH

CAN WE DANCE?

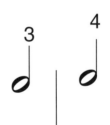

RH
4 3 4 3   2   2   2   3   4   4

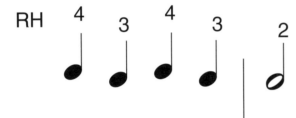
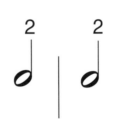

LH
2 3 2 3   4   4   4   3 4   4

Can you play this *3 times* on *3 different groups of black keys*?

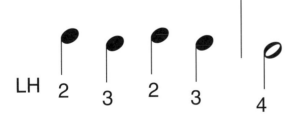

WHOLE NOTE

A **WHOLE NOTE** is a very **LONG** note. We give it **FOUR** counts.

Clap: | Count:

Clap:	♩	♩	♩	♩	♩	♩	♩	♩	♩	♩	♩	♩
Count:	1	2	3	4	1	2	3	4	1	2	3	4

Middle

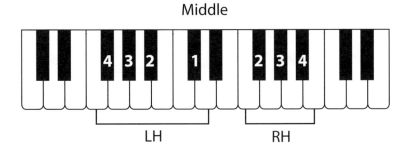

LH   RH

BRAVO BOX

9. Good hand position

10. Steady tempo and counting

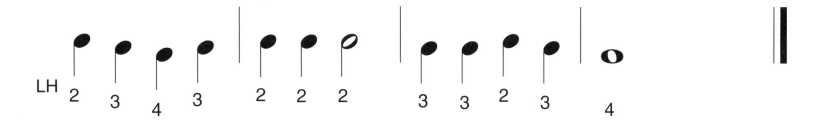

MERRILY

Traditional

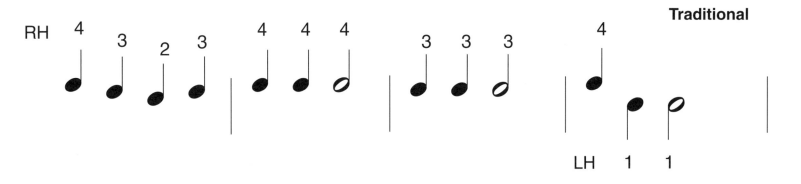

Middle

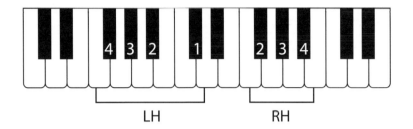

LH   RH

BRAVO BOX

11. Good hand position

12. Steady tempo and counting

A WINDY DAY

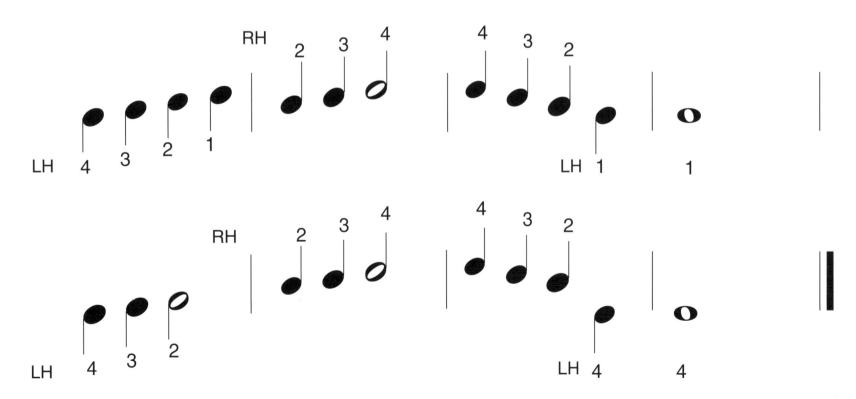

Dynamic signs tell us how loudly or softly we should play.
FORTE is the Italian word for **LOUD**.
This sign tells us to play **LOUDLY**.

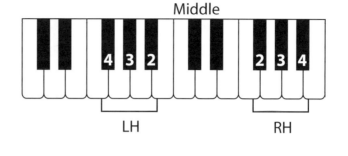

Middle

LH   RH

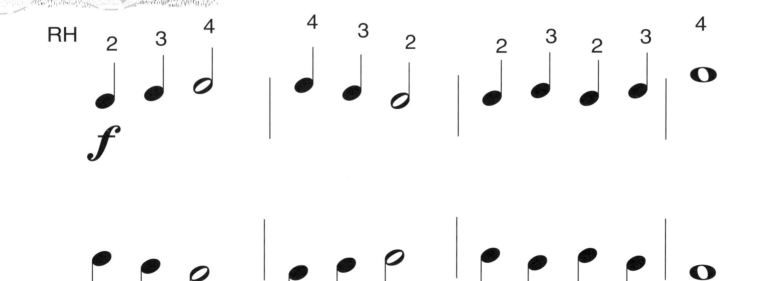

THUNDER!

f

_p_
PIANO OR **SOFT**

PIANO is the Italian word for **SOFT**. This sign tells us to play **SOFTLY**.

Middle

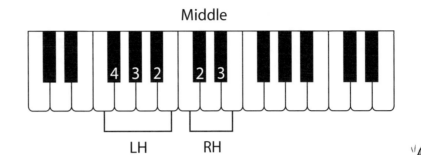

LH   RH

BRAVO BOX

16. Good hand position

17. Steady tempo and counting

18. Play softly

WHISPERS!

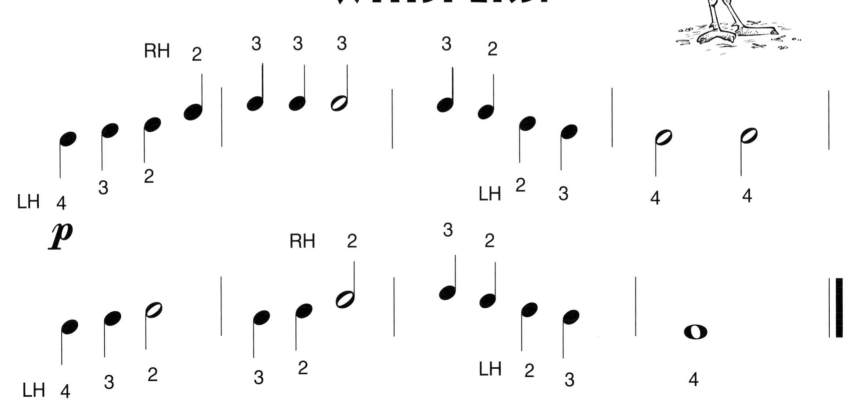

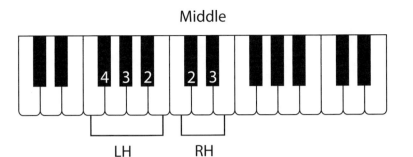

Middle

WAS THAT AN ECHO?

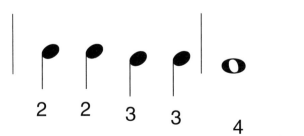

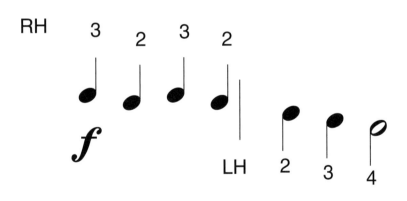

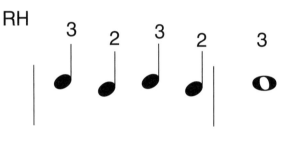

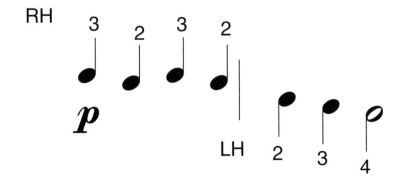

THE MUSIC ALPHABET

Count the number of **WHITE KEYS** on your piano keyboard and write your answer below.

There are_____ **WHITE KEYS** on my piano.

Each **WHITE KEY** on the keyboard is named with a letter of the alphabet.

The music alphabet has only **SEVEN LETTERS:**   **A   B   C   D   E   F   G**

If you look at a group of **THREE BLACK KEYS**, you can see where **A** is:

B is right next to A, just like in the alphabet:

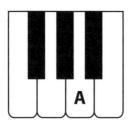

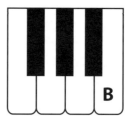

Starting at the bottom of the keyboard find all the A's.

Find all the **B's** on the keyboard. How many are there?

There are_____ **A's** on the keyboard.

There are_____ **B's** on the keyboard.

C is next to B. If you look at a group of **TWO BLACK KEYS**, you can see where **C** is:

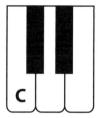

Find all the **C**'s on the keyboard.
How many are there?

There are _____ **C**'s on the keyboard.

E is next to D:

Find all the **E's** on the keyboard.
How many are there?

There are _____ **E's** on the keyboard.

G is next to F:

D is next to C:

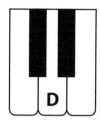

Find all the **D's** on the keyboard.
How many are there?

There are _____ **D's** on the keyboard.

F is next to E. If you look at a group of **THREE BLACK KEYS**, you can see where **F** is:

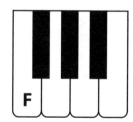

Find all the **F's** on the keyboard.
How many are there?

There are _____ **F's** on the keyboard.

Find all the **G's** on the keyboard. How many are there?

There are _____ **G's** on the keyboard.

MIDDLE C is the C closest to the **MIDDLE** of the keyboard. You will usually find it below the piano's nameplate.

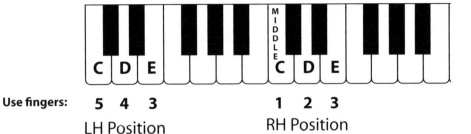

Use fingers: **5 4 3**   **1 2 3**

LH Position   RH Position

THE CAROUSEL

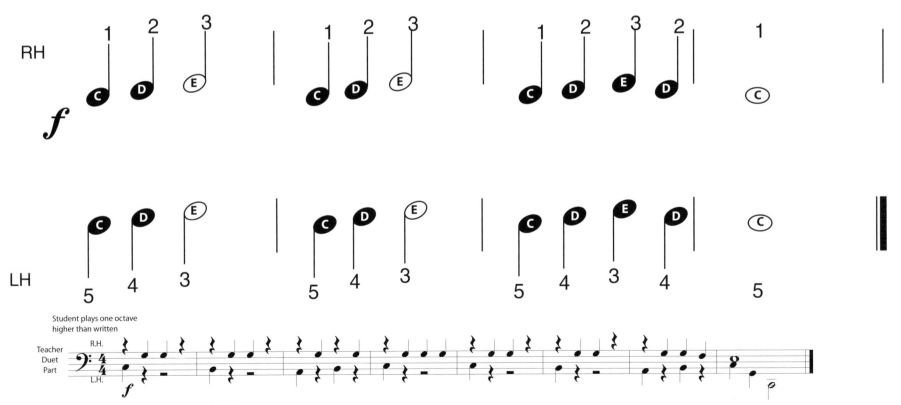

Student plays one octave higher than written

Teacher Duet Part

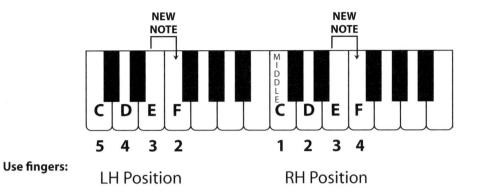

Use fingers:

LH Position   RH Position

BRAVO BOX

21. Steady tempo and counting

22. Dynamic contrasts

Name all notes aloud before you begin practicing each day. Then sing the note names as you play the 1st time through.

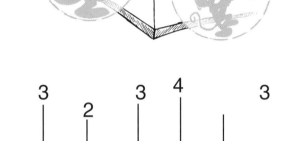

HIDE AND SEEK!

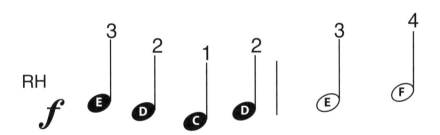

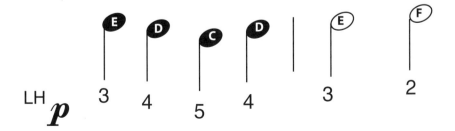

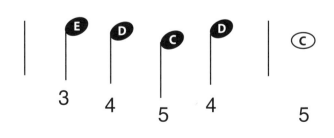

REPEAT SIGN

The **REPEAT SIGN** tells us to play the section again.

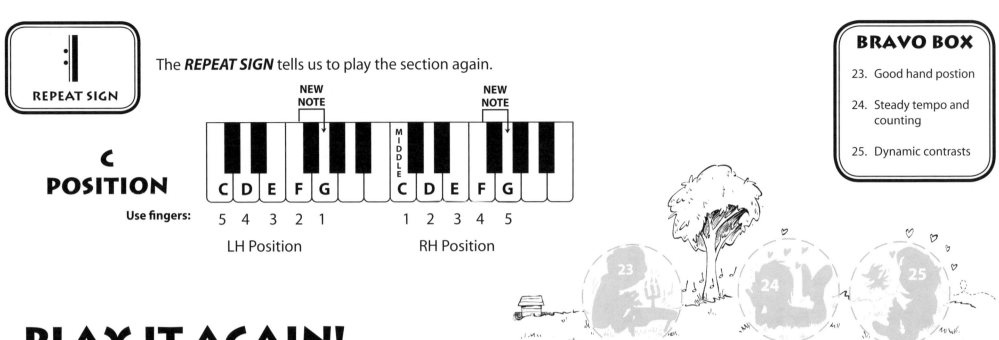

C POSITION

Use fingers:

NEW NOTE   NEW NOTE

5 4 3 2 1   1 2 3 4 5

LH Position   RH Position

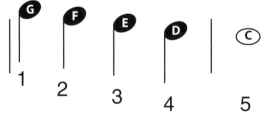

PLAY IT AGAIN!

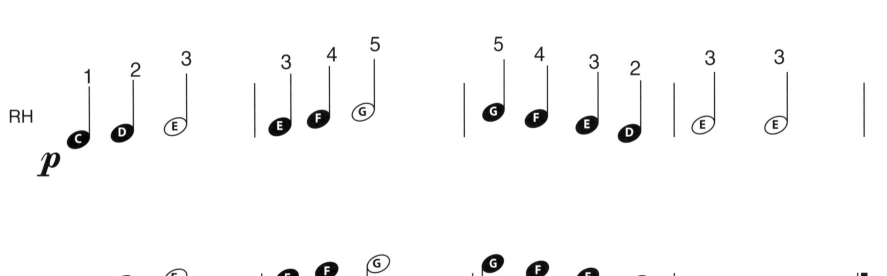

RH

p

LH

f

4/4 TIME SIGNATURE

A *TIME SIGNATURE* usually appears at the beginning of a piece of music.

4 The top *FOUR* tells us that there are *FOUR* counts in each measure.

4 The bottom *FOUR* tells us that each *QUARTER NOTE* (♩) receives *ONE* count.

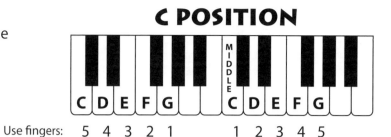

C POSITION

Use fingers: 5 4 3 2 1   1 2 3 4 5

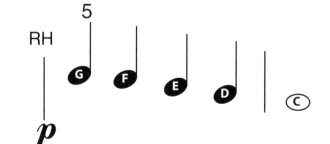

MIRROR IMAGES

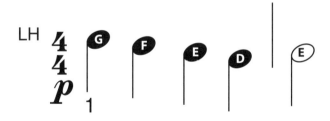

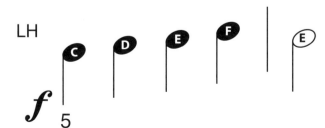
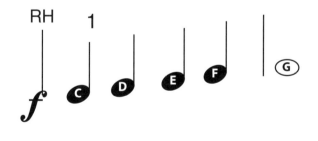

C POSITION

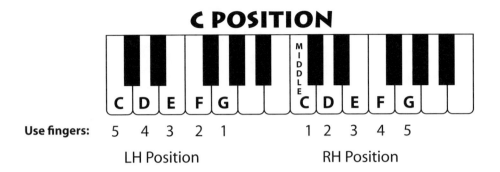

Use fingers: 5 4 3 2 1   1 2 3 4 5

LH Position   RH Position

BRAVO BOX

29. Good hand position

30. Steady tempo and counting

31. Dynamic contrasts

LIGHTLY ROW

Traditional

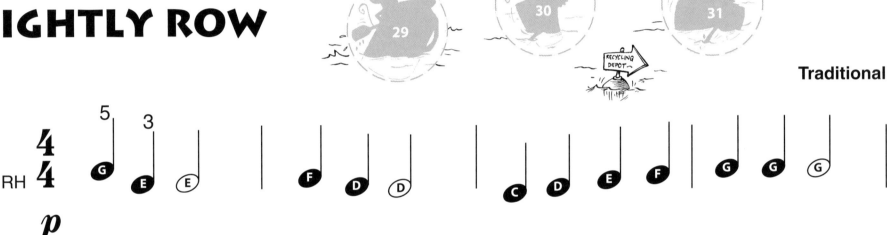

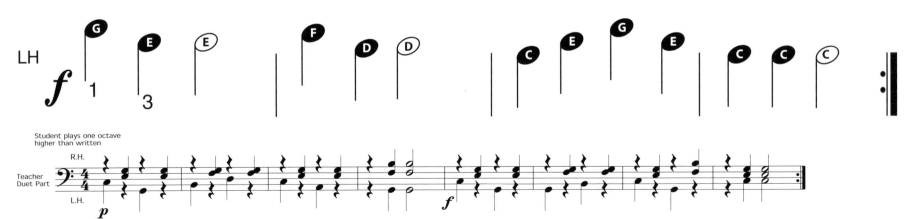

<table>
<tr><td>**2
4**
TIME SIGNATURE</td><td>**2** tells us that there are **TWO** counts in each measure.

4 tells us that each **QUARTER NOTE** (♩) receives **ONE** count.</td></tr>
</table>

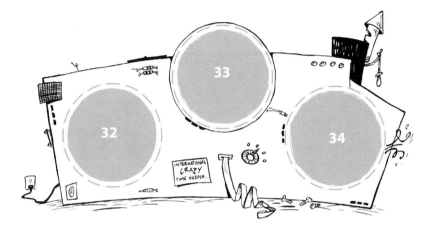

Name all notes aloud before you begin practicing each day. Then sing the note names as you play the 1st time through.

WHAT TIME IS IT?

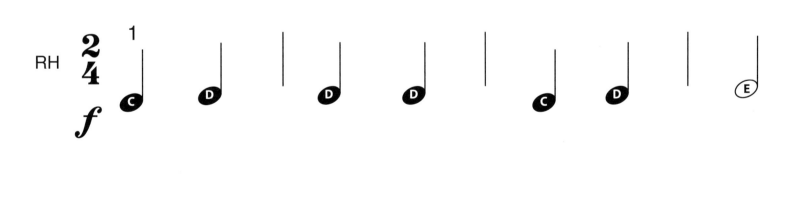

GONE FISHIN'!

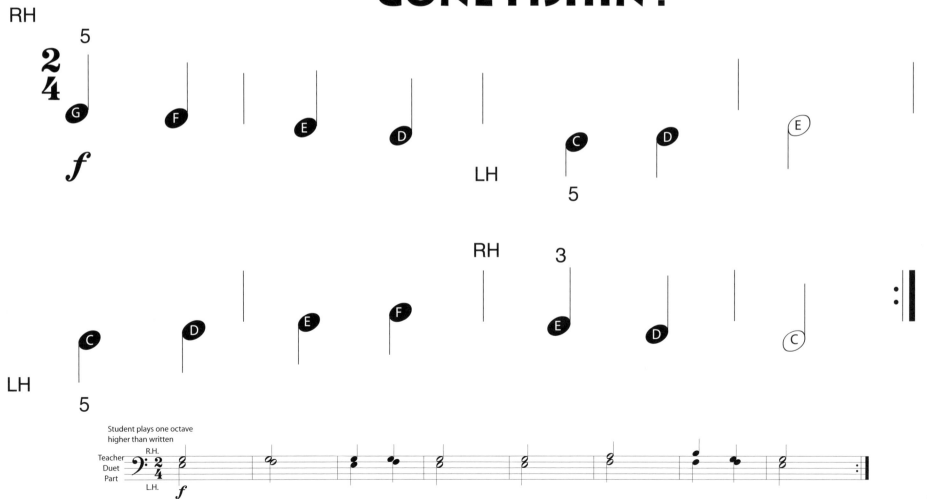

3 tells us that there are **THREE** counts in each measure.

4 tells us that each **QUARTER NOTE** (♩) receives **ONE** count.

A **DOTTED HALF NOTE** is a **LONG** note.
We give it **THREE** counts.

BRAVO BOX

36. Good hand position

37. Steady tempo and counting

38. Dynamic contrasts

SKIPPING ALONG

TADPOLE FISHING

BRAVO BOX

39. Good hand position

40. Steady tempo and counting

41. Dynamic contrasts

Name all notes aloud before you begin practicing each day. Then sing the note names as you play the 1st time through.

THE MUSIC STAFF

The music staff has 5 **LINES**...    ...and 4 **SPACES**.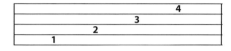

Notes are written on the lines. 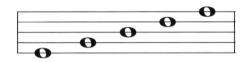   Notes are written in the spaces.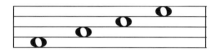

This is called a
TREBLE CLEF or
G CLEF.

The treble clef tells us to play **HIGH NOTES** above middle C.

We usually use our **RIGHT HAND** when we are told to play in the treble clef.

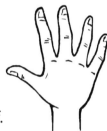

This is called a
BASS CLEF or
F CLEF.

The bass clef tells us to play **LOW NOTES** below middle C.

We usually use our **LEFT HAND** when we are told to play in the bass clef.

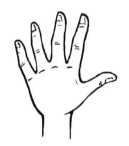

Middle C can be played with either the **RIGHT HAND** or the **LEFT HAND**.

1. Circle all the **SPACE** notes in **GREEN**.
2. Circle all the **LINE** notes in **BLUE**.

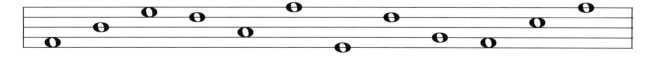

RIGHT HAND
C D E

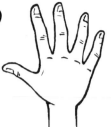

RH POSITION

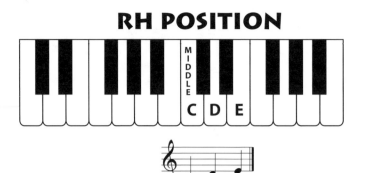

Use fingers: 1   2   3

Treble Clef

BRAVO BOX

42. Steady tempo and counting

Name all notes aloud before you begin practicing each day. Then sing the note names as you play the 1st time through.

C, D & E?

DO YOU KNOW C, D & E?

Steadily → A tempo or mood marking usually appears at the beginning of a piece of music. It tells us at what speed or in what mood the piece is to be played.

f   C   D   E   E   D   C   Do   you   know   them   well?

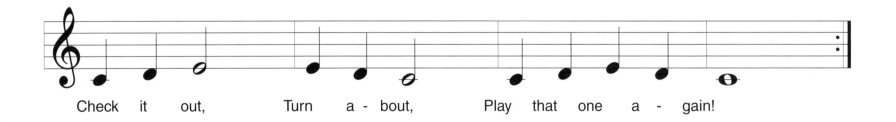

Check   it   out,   Turn   a - bout,   Play   that   one   a - gain!

12271

REPEATED NOTES

Notes are **REPEATED** when they follow each other in the same line or space.

play again

play again

STEPS

Notes move **BY STEP** when they follow each other from **LINE** to **SPACE** or **SPACE** to **LINE**. Notes can move **UP** or **DOWN** by step.

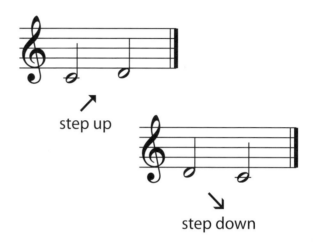

step up

step down

Name all notes aloud before you begin practicing each day. Then sing the note names as you play the 1st time through.

A HORSEBACK RIDE

Happily

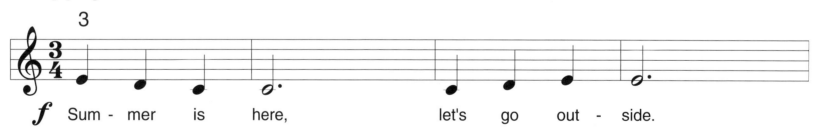

f Sum - mer is here, let's go out - side.

TREASURE HUNT

Find all the **REPEATED** notes in this piece.

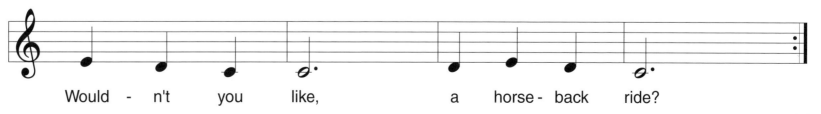

Would - n't you like, a horse - back ride?

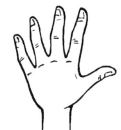

LEFT HAND C D E

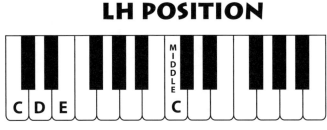

LH POSITION

C D E ... MIDDLE C

Use fingers: 5 4 3

BRAVO BOX

45. Steady tempo and counting

Name all notes aloud before you begin practicing each day. Then sing the note names as you play the 1st time through.

Bass Clef

45

I CAN PLAY!

Steadily

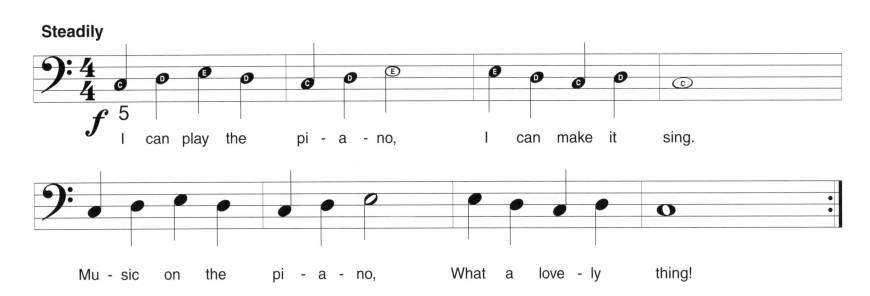

I can play the pi - a - no, I can make it sing.

Mu - sic on the pi - a - no, What a love - ly thing!

In this piece, do you notice that some of the stems point **UP** and some of the stems point **DOWN**?

The stems go **DOWN** when the note is **ABOVE** the middle line.

The stems go **UP** when the note is **BELOW** the middle line.

The stems can go **UP** or **DOWN** when the note is on the middle line.

REPEATED NOTES

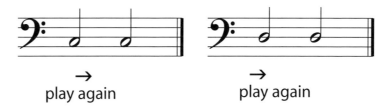

→ play again

→ play again

STEPS

↓ step down

↗ step up

BRAVO BOX

46. Good hand position

47. Steady tempo and counting

Name all notes aloud before you begin practicing each day. Then sing the note names as you play the 1st time through.

ALL BY MYSELF!

Moderately

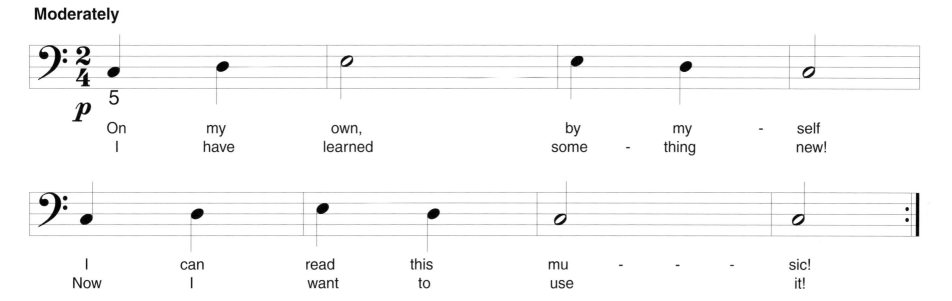

On   my   own,   by   my - self
I   have   learned   some - thing   new!

I   can   read   this   mu - - - sic!
Now   I   want   to   use   it!

Student plays one octave higher than written

Teacher Duet Part

TREASURE HUNT
Find all the **REPEATED** notes in this piece.

RIGHT HAND C POSITION

TUM DI DUM

Steadily

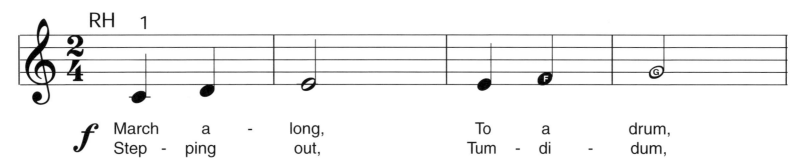

Use fingers: 1 2 3 4 5

NEW NOTES

Name all notes aloud before you begin practicing each day. Then sing the note names as you play the 1st time through.

RH 1

$\boldsymbol{f}$

March   a   -   long,   To   a   drum,
Step - ping   out,   Tum - di   -   dum,

5

March - ing   is   such   good   fun!
March - ing   in   the   warm   sun!

BRAVO BOX

50. Name all notes aloud

51. Good hand position

52. Steady tempo and counting

Name all notes aloud before you begin practicing each day. Then sing the note names as you play the 1st time through.

THE SWIMMING LESSON

Moderately

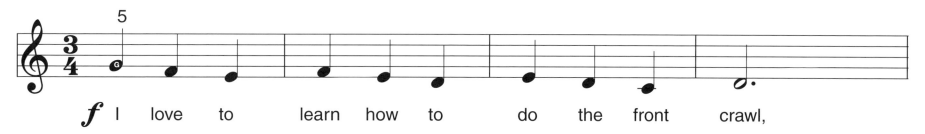

f I love to learn how to do the front crawl,

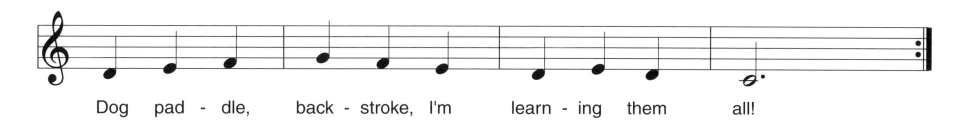

Dog pad - dle, back - stroke, I'm learn - ing them all!

𝄢 LEFT HAND C POSITION

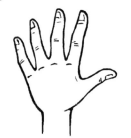

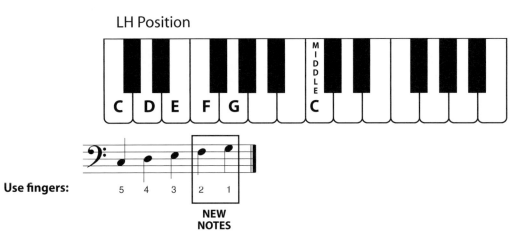

LH Position

C D E F G MIDDLE C

Use fingers: 5 4 3 2 1

NEW NOTES

LEFT HAND FUN!

Steadily

𝑓 Walk- ing up to G, Then back down to C!

By the left, hap - pi - ly, Fun for you and me!

ROLLERBLADING

Moderately

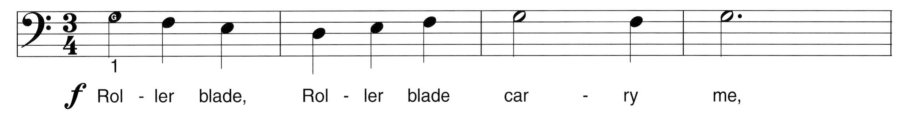

f Rol - ler blade, Rol - ler blade car - ry me,

Up and down, Up and down my fav - orite street!

THE GRAND STAFF

When the **TREBLE CLEF** and the **BASS STAFF** are joined together it is called the **GRAND STAFF**.

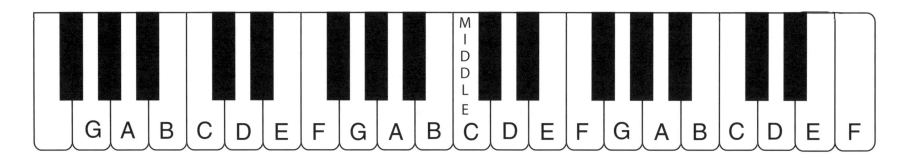

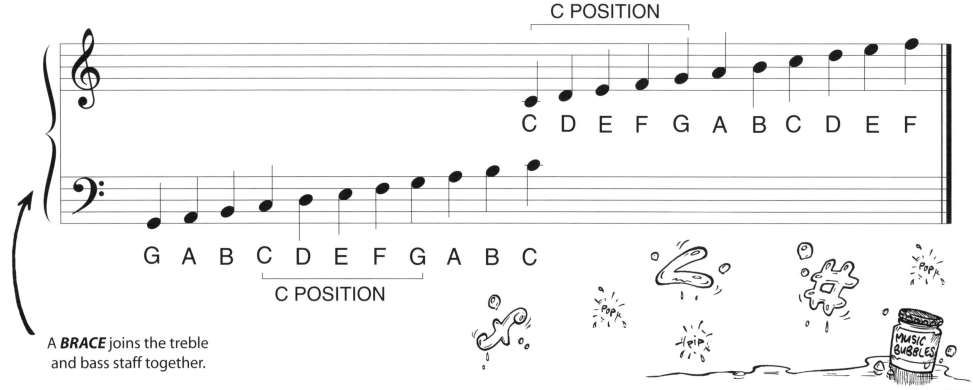

A **BRACE** joins the treble and bass staff together.

12271

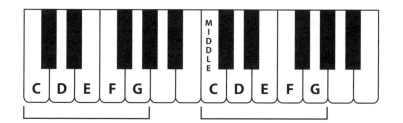

C POSITION

Name all notes aloud before you begin practicing each day. Then sing the note names as you play the 1st time through.

BRAVO BOX

58. Steady tempo and counting

59. Dynamic contrasts

LET'S MARCH TOGETHER!

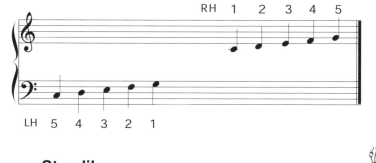

RH 1 2 3 4 5

LH 5 4 3 2 1

Steadily

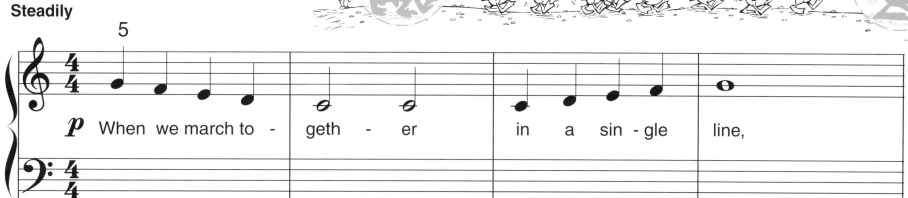

5

p When we march to - geth - er in a sin - gle line,

f We can march much bet - ter, We can look so fine!

1

TREASURE HUNT
Find all the **REPEATED NOTES** in this piece.

BRAVO BOX

60. Good hand position

61. Dynamic contrasts

Name all notes aloud before you begin practicing each day. Then sing the note names as you play the 1st time through.

CAN YOU REPEAT THAT?

Are you remembering to watch your music, not your hands?

Moderately

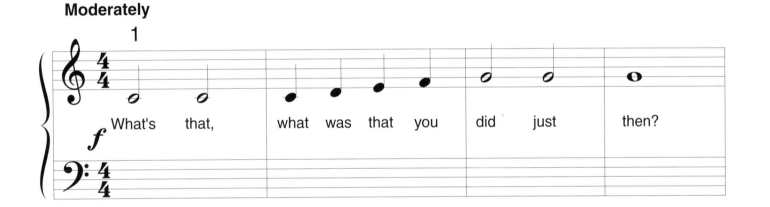

What's that, what was that you did just then?

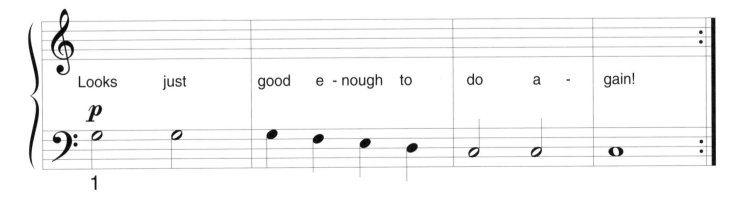

Looks just good e - nough to do a - gain!

TREASURE HUNT
Find all the
notes which
STEP DOWN.

BRAVO BOX

62. Steady tempo and
counting

*Name all notes aloud
before you begin practicing
each day. Then sing the
note names as you play the
1st time through.*

A SURPRISE PACKAGE!

Happily

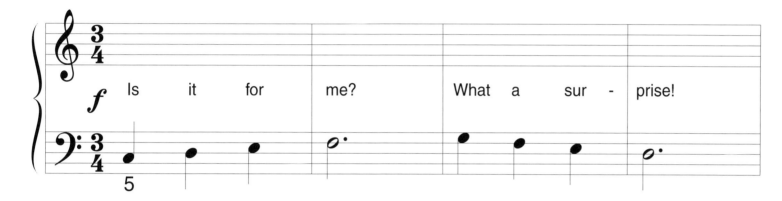

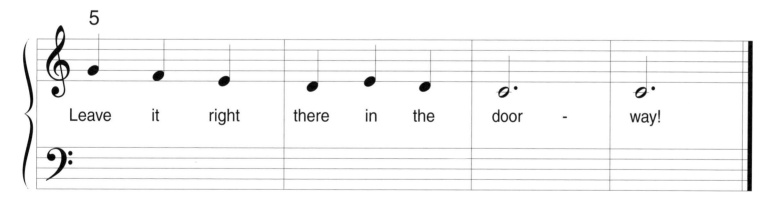

SLUR OR PHRASE

This is a **SLUR or PHRASE** and can be placed above or below a group of two or more notes. It divides the notes into musical "sentences" or "phrases" and tells us to play **LEGATO** (an Italian word meaning smoothly connected).

BRAVO BOX

63. Good hand position

64. Smooth phrases

65. Dynamic contrasts

RIDING MY BIKE

Name all notes aloud before you begin practicing each day. Then sing the note names as you play the 1st time through.

Smoothly

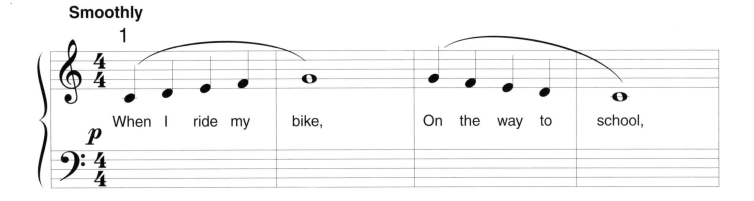

When I ride my bike, On the way to school,

TREASURE HUNT Find all the **HALF NOTES** in this piece.

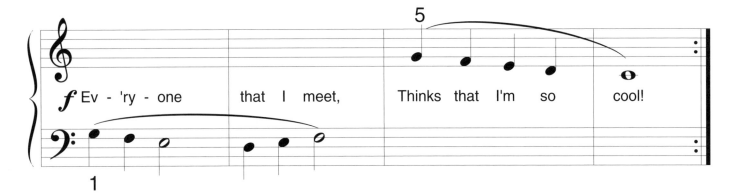

Ev - 'ry - one that I meet, Thinks that I'm so cool!

Name all notes aloud before you begin practicing each day. Then sing the note names as you play the 1st time through.

A CAMPING SONG

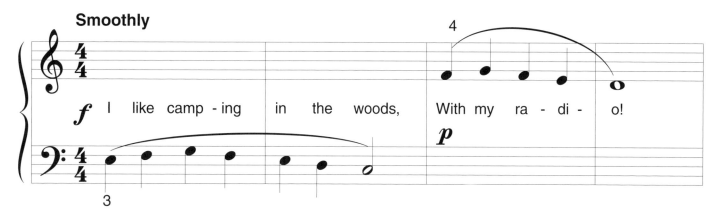

TREASURE HUNT

Find all the notes which **STEP UP**.

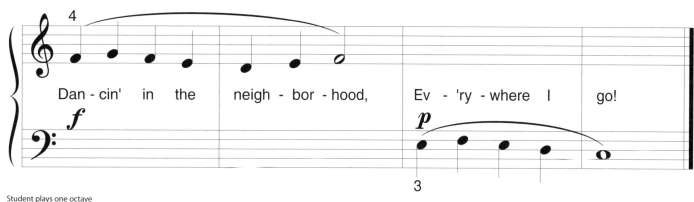

Student plays one octave higher than written

Teacher Duet Part

QUARTER REST

A **QUARTER REST** means **ONE** count or beat of silence.

A PUPPET DANCE

Name all notes aloud before you begin practicing each day. Then sing the note names as you play the 1st time through.

Moderately

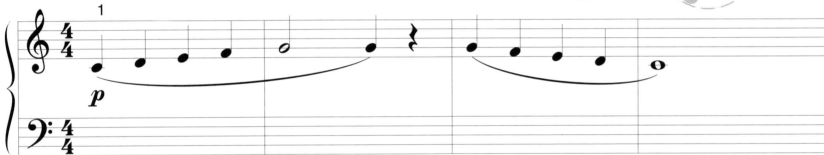

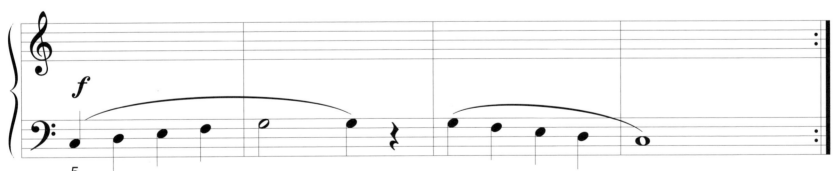

Student plays one octave higher than written

Teacher Duet Part

TREASURE HUNT

How many **QUARTER RESTS** can you find in this piece?

12271

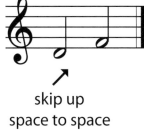

skip up
line to line

skip down
space to space

skip up
space to space

skip down
line to line

Name all notes aloud before you begin practicing each day. Then sing the note names as you play the 1st time through.

SKIP THIS!

Smoothly

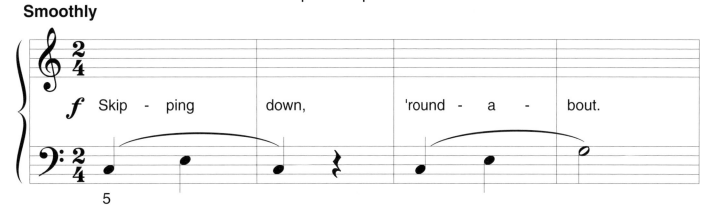

Skip - ping   down,   'round - a - bout.

5

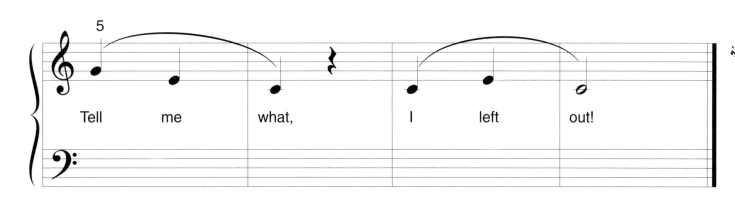

Tell   me   what,   I   left   out!

TREASURE HUNT

How many **SKIPS** are there in this piece?

HALF REST

A **HALF REST** means **TWO** counts or beats of silence.

BRAVO BOX

72. Steady tempo and counting

73. Dynamic contrasts

Name all notes aloud before you begin practicing each day. Then sing the note names as you play the 1st time through.

WIND-UP TOYS

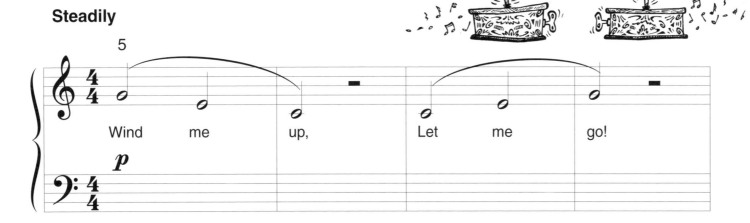

Steadily

5

Wind   me   up,   Let   me   go!

p

TREASURE HUNT
How many **HALF RESTS** can you find in this piece?

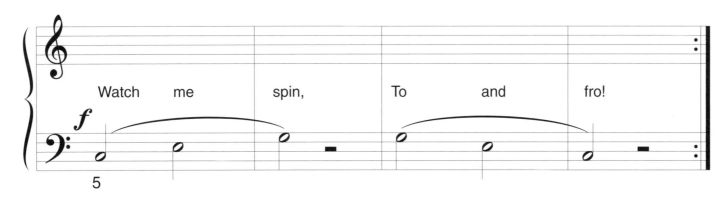

Watch   me   spin,   To   and   fro!

f

5

THE DANCING BEARS

BRAVO BOX

74. Smooth phrases

75. Dynamic contrasts

Name all notes aloud before you begin practicing each day. Then sing the note names as you play the 1st time through.

Smoothly

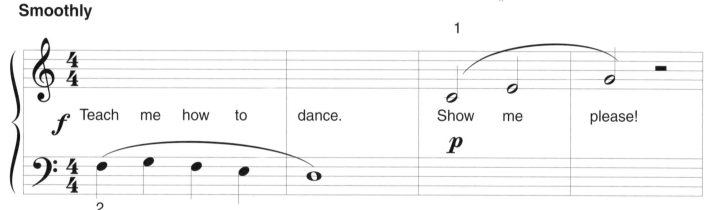

f Teach me how to dance. Show me please!

p

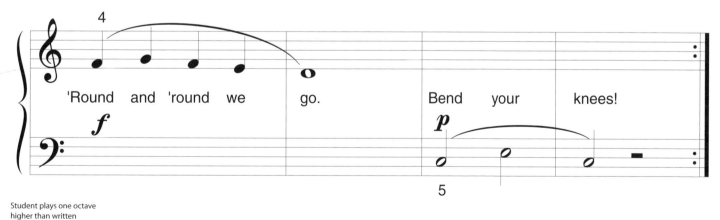

'Round and 'round we go. Bend your knees!

f p

TREASURE HUNT
Find all the notes which **SKIP** in this piece.

Student plays one octave higher than written

Teacher Duet Part

WHOLE REST

A **WHOLE REST** means the **ENTIRE BAR OR MEASURE** is silent. (It does not matter what the time signature is.) The top number of the time signature will tell you how long (how many counts) to rest.

BRAVO BOX

76. Good hand position

77. Steady tempo and counting

LET'S WAIT AROUND!

Name all notes aloud before you begin practicing each day. Then sing the note names as you play the 1st time through.

Steadily

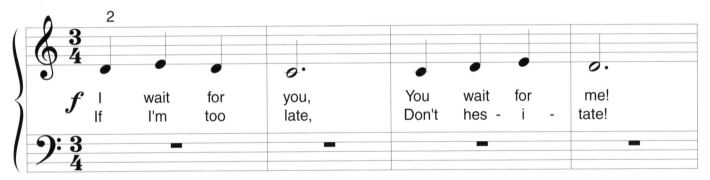

I wait for you,
If I'm too late,

You wait for me!
Don't hes - i - tate!

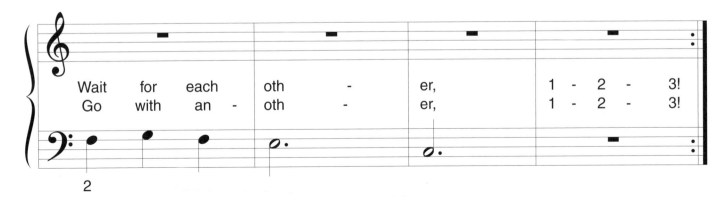

Wait for each oth - er,
Go with an - oth - er,

1 - 2 - 3!
1 - 2 - 3!

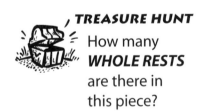
TREASURE HUNT
How many **WHOLE RESTS** are there in this piece?

MY DOG 'BILL'

Smoothly

BRAVO BOX

78. Smooth phrases

79. Dynamic contrasts

Name all notes aloud before you begin practicing each day. Then sing the note names as you play the 1st time through.

TREASURE HUNT Find all the notes which **SKIP** in this piece.

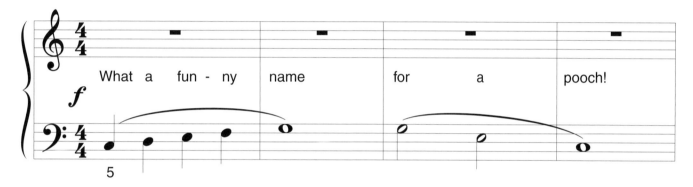

What a fun - ny name   for   a   pooch!

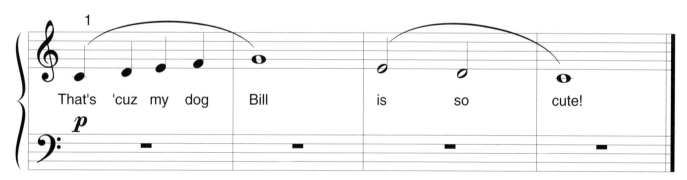

That's 'cuz my dog   Bill   is   so   cute!

Student plays one octave higher than written

Teacher Duet Part

CERTIFICATE OF ACCOMPLISHMENT

Congratulations to

80

_____
(name of student)

for successfully completing
Preparatory Level A of Beanstalk's Basics for Piano.
You are now promoted to **Preparatory Level B**.

DATE: _____   TEACHER: _____